Essential Lives

Frederick Douglass

Essential Lives

Frederick Douglass

Fugitive Slave & Abolitionist

By Sue Vander Hook

Content Consultant:
Kira Duke, Education Program Manager
National Civil Rights Museum

ABDO
Publishing Company

CREDITS

Published by ABDO Publishing Company, 8000 West 78th Street, Edina, Minnesota 55439.

Printed in the United States.
052010
092010

 THIS BOOK CONTAINS AT LEAST 10% RECYCLED MATERIALS.

Editor: Nadia Higgins
Copy Editor: Nicholas Cafarelli
Interior Design and Production: Christa Schneider
Cover Design: Christa Schneider

Library of Congress Cataloging-in-Publication Data
Vander Hook, Sue, 1949–
Frederick Douglass : fugitive slave and abolitionist / Sue Vander Hook.
p. cm. — (Essential lives)
Includes bibliographical references and index.
ISBN 978-1-61613-513-3
1. Douglass, Frederick, 1818–1895—Juvenile literature. 2. Abolitionists—United States—Biography—Juvenile literature. 3. African American abolitionists—Biography—Juvenile literature. 4. Antislavery movements—United States—Juvenile literature. I. Title.
E449.D75V36 2011
973.8092—dc22
[B]

2010000531

TABLE OF CONTENTS

Chapter 1	*The Slave Breaker*	6
Chapter 2	*Born a Slave*	14
Chapter 3	*The Slave and the Whip*	24
Chapter 4	*Baltimore*	34
Chapter 5	*Motivated to Learn*	42
Chapter 6	*Return to Slavery*	50
Chapter 7	*Escape to New York*	60
Chapter 8	*Popular Orator*	70
Chapter 9	*War!*	80
Chapter 10	*Milestones*	88
Timeline		96
Essential Facts		100
Additional Resources		102
Glossary		104
Source Notes		106
Index		110
About the Author		112

Chapter 1

Douglass was born in Talbot County, Maryland. His youth was divided between towns in that county and Baltimore.

The Slave Breaker

It was New Year's Day, 1834. Sixteen-year-old Frederick Bailey set out on foot early that blustery, cold morning. His journey would take him seven miles (11.3 km) along Maryland's beautiful shoreline. His rutted path was on the jagged eastern shore of the Chesapeake Bay, where the Delmarva Peninsula juts into the Atlantic Ocean.

Frederick was traveling by himself, an unusual thing for a black man, especially a slave who might try to escape. But chances were slim that Frederick would find a way off the peninsula. And even if he did slip away to a free Northern state, he would surely be captured and returned to his owner.

Maryland

The state of Maryland, where Frederick Douglass was born, lies on the East Coast and is split down the middle by the Chesapeake Bay. Land east of the bay on the Delmarva Peninsula is commonly called the Eastern Shore. Maryland shares the peninsula with the state of Delaware. Maryland acquired slaves shortly after the colony was established in 1634.

Breaking Spirits

Frederick trudged ahead, his destination a farm that filled his heart with dread and made his mind race with fear. For the next year he would work for Edward Covey, a white man who rented and farmed the fertile land. Covey had a reputation as one of the best professional slave breakers around. He could take a slave owner's most rebellious slave, break the slave's spirit, and force the slave to obey. Frederick later wrote, "Like a wild young working animal, I am to be broken to the yoke of a bitter and life-long bondage."[1]

It usually took approximately a year for Covey to "knock sense" into a stubborn slave. Covey received no money for his services. Instead, for a year he had a free farmhand—one he could abuse and overwork as much as he wanted. And, when Covey was done, the slave owner was pleased to have a very submissive slave returned to him.

Covey was also well known for his skillful and frequent use of a whip. Frederick had heard about Covey's lashes and witnessed the welts and scars on the backs of returning slaves. Frederick had never been whipped himself, but now he was terrified of the inevitable lashing.

The Oxen and the Cart

When Frederick arrived at the farm, he saw a small house badly worn by the damp, saltwater air. On one side churned the white, foamy waters of the Chesapeake Bay. On the other were thick pine forests and farmland. The setting was beautiful, but to Frederick, it was a foreboding scene.

The first of many clashes with Covey took place on Frederick's third day at the farm. At daybreak on January 3, Covey ordered Frederick to take the ox-drawn cart into the forest and gather wood.

The two huge beasts—Buck and Darby—were not fully trained, and Frederick knew nothing about handling oxen. Covey gave him a quick lesson in commands. Then he tied a rope around Buck's horn and gave the other end to Frederick. Covey told him to never let go of the rope, even if the oxen should bolt and run. In that case, Frederick must hold on and pull until the oxen stopped.

Frederick held firmly to the rope, afraid to disobey this cruel man. With rope in hand, Frederick ran

Slavery in the United States

Before the Civil War (1861–1865), slavery was legal in the United States. Ninety-five percent of the nation's slaves lived in the South, where plantations of all sizes depended on slave labor. Some states that bordered the South, such as Missouri, Kentucky, Delaware, and Maryland, also considered slavery normal and necessary.

Most slaves worked in fields, planting and harvesting cotton, rice, corn, sugarcane, and tobacco. Others worked as carpenters, blacksmiths, drivers, and stable hands. Domestic servants worked in the main house, serving the plantation's master and his family. They cleaned, cooked, sewed, and cared for the slave owner's children. Their living conditions were often better than the field slaves, who usually lacked adequate quarters, food, and clothing. Slaves were considered property, owned primarily by wealthy white landowners. As the nation expanded west, the question of whether slavery should be legal in new states became an issue. Abolitionists—people who wanted to abolish, or end, slavery—worked hard to keep slavery out of new states and to make it illegal in existing states. They also created a complex secret system, called the Underground Railroad, that provided escape routes for slaves who wanted to flee to free Northern states and Canada.

In His Own Words

In 1845, seven years after his escape, Frederick Douglass wrote *Narrative of the Life of Frederick Douglass, an American Slave*. It was the first of three autobiographies. In it he described his life as a slave and a fugitive. The book became a bestseller and helped spark the abolitionist movement of the nineteenth century.

alongside the oxen as they pulled the cart quickly across the open field. He managed to hang on even when the oxen were spooked and dashed madly away. But then the animals crashed into a tree, and the wheels of the cart flew off. The oxen were tangled in a group of saplings, furious that they could not wiggle loose. Frederick frantically tried to fix the mess. He put the cart back together and cut down the small trees that trapped the oxen.

The stunned animals now moved slowly to the woodpile, and Frederick filled the cart with firewood. Then he headed back to the farmhouse only to once again meet with disaster. When the gate to the farm was in sight, the oxen took off at full speed with the cart twisting and turning behind them. Afraid he would be crushed by one of the gateposts, Frederick let go of the rope. The cart hit the gate and shattered.

Broken in Body, Soul, and Spirit

Covey was watching with rage in his eyes. In a voice like a growling dog, he snarled, "Go back to the woods again."[2] Frederick obeyed, but this time Covey came along. In the forest, the slave breaker ordered Frederick to stop the oxen. Then he cut off three slender tree shoots and trimmed them with his knife. He ordered Frederick to take off his clothes, but the young slave refused. Then Covey rushed at him with "the savage fierceness of a wolf" and tore off Frederick's well-worn clothing.[3]

What followed was a whipping—Frederick's first—that made his back bleed and swell with crisscrossing rows of puffy welts. The brutal whipping damaged Frederick's body and demoralized his spirit. He later wrote, "Mr. Covey succeeded in breaking me. I was broken in body, soul, and spirit; . . . the dark night of slavery closed in upon me!"[4]

It was the first of many weekly beatings Frederick would endure. He later recalled:

> *If at any one time of my life, more than another, I was made to drink the bitterest dregs of slavery, that time was during the first six months of my stay with Mr. Covey.*[5]

> *. . . I was completely wrecked, changed and bewildered; goaded almost to madness at one time, and at another reconciling myself to my wretched condition.*[6]

Undying Hope

Although Covey broke Frederick's will, he could not shatter his hope. Frederick never stopped dreaming of freedom and longing for a chance to escape. When sailboats passed by on the Chesapeake Bay, he thought,

> *You [boats] are loosed from your moorings, and free; I am fast in my chains, and am a slave! You move merrily before the gentle gale, and I sadly before the bloody whip! You are freedom's swift-winged angels, that fly around the world; I am confined in bands of iron! O, that I were free!* [7]

Four years later, Frederick Bailey would disguise himself as a sailor, board a train, and escape from slavery. He would live as a fugitive under an assumed name—Frederick Douglass—to avoid being captured and returned to his owner.

Frederick Douglass would eventually become a symbol of slavery as well as an icon of freedom. He would dedicate his life to abolishing slavery and exposing the injustice of humans owning other humans. Motivated by an undying passion, he would one day see his people—all black slaves—living free.

> "It may be that my misery in slavery will only increase my happiness when I get free. There is a better day coming."[8]
>
> —*Frederick Douglass*

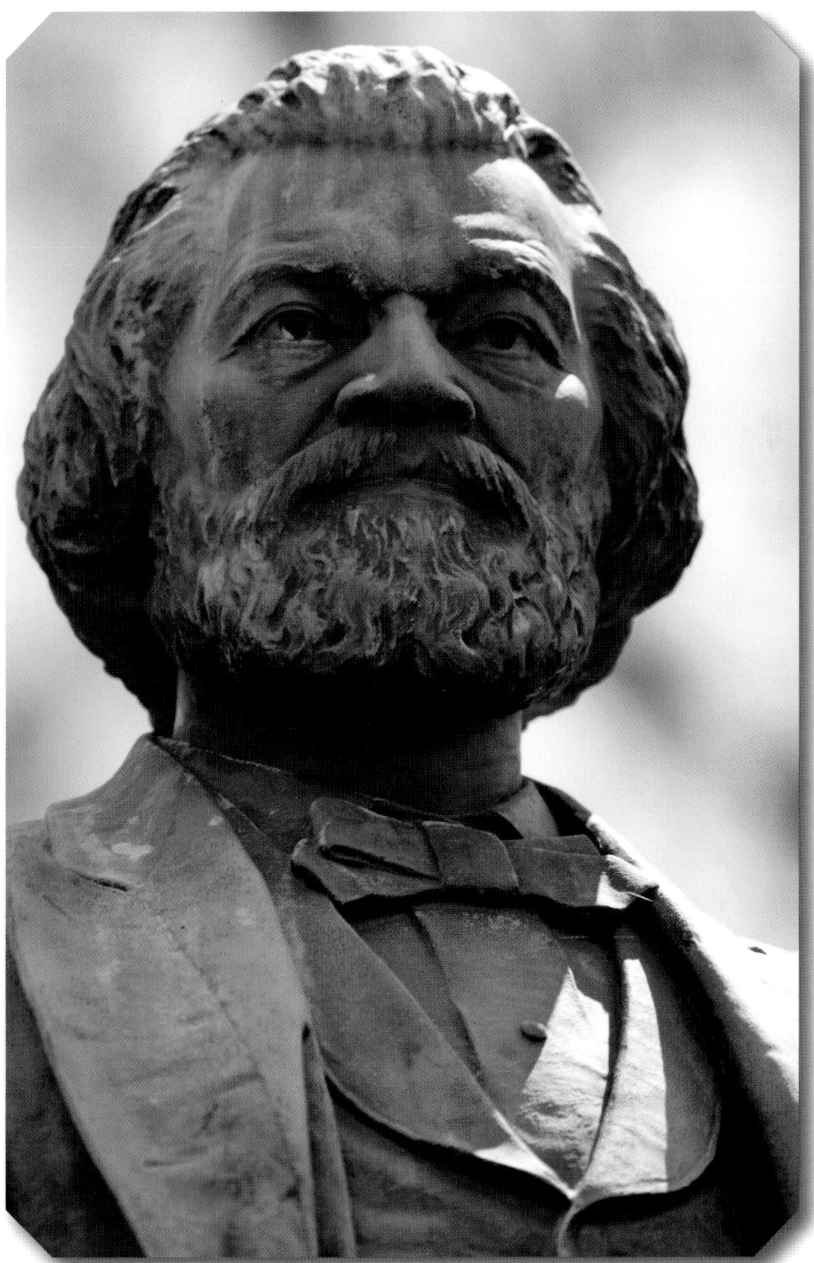

In 1899, a statue of Frederick Douglass was erected in Rochester, New York. It was the first U.S. monument to ever honor an African American.

Chapter 2

Frederick's first home was a simple log cabin.

Born a Slave

Frederick Augustus Washington Bailey was born in February 1818 at Holmes Hill Farm in Talbot County, Maryland. His mother was Harriet Bailey, a young black slave. Frederick received his mother's surname, as his father was unknown. Or perhaps, as rumor had it, his father was a white man, possibly Aaron Anthony, their master. Anthony was the plantation manager for Edward Lloyd, one of the wealthiest men in Maryland.

No one knew the exact day Frederick was born. That was not unusual for slaves, whose birthdays typically were not recorded.

Slave Auctions

Before the Civil War, slave auctions in the South were advertised weeks in advance. Buyers from all over inspected the slaves—hundreds of men, women, and children. The buyers treated the slaves like animals, checking their teeth and muscles. The slaves were displayed on the auction block and sold to the highest bidder. A strong young black man in his prime was sold for as much as $1,600 (about $35,000 today). Sales for a typical two-day auction with 400 slaves totaled more than $300,000 (nearly $7 million today).

The Bailey Family

Frederick was a fifth-generation Bailey in America; the first had arrived in Maryland in the early 1700s. The Baileys were fortunate to have kept their family together for more than a century. In the Deep South, slaves were often sold at slave auctions and separated from family members forever.

Frederick had a large family. It included his grandparents, Betsey and Isaac Bailey; many aunts and uncles; scores of cousins; his mother; and three siblings, Perry, Sarah, and Eliza. By the time he turned four, Frederick would have two more sisters,

Kitty and Arianna. Harriet was allowed to raise her babies until they were no longer nursing. Then, her mother, Betsey, took over, and Harriet was sent to an outlying farm to work in the fields.

Frederick's memory of his mother was hazy. He remembered her as "tall and finely proportioned, of dark, glossy complexion, with regular features." He recalled that "amongst the slaves [she] was remarkably sedate and dignified."[1] Apparently, his mother could read, which was quite an unusual achievement for a slave and a skill she probably kept quiet. Teaching a slave to read and write was illegal because literacy might teach a slave to become disobedient and therefore worthless. Even worse, a literate slave might plot an escape or stir up a revolt.

Cabin by the Creek

Frederick's home was a small log cabin near Tuckahoe Creek, a brook that flowed through nearby farm fields. Maryland's rich farmland on the Delmarva Peninsula was fed by numerous brooks and rivers. Frederick's grandmother, Betsey, fished regularly in those creeks.

The Bailey cabin was humble and meager, with packed-clay floors, a mud chimney, and no windows.

Living in a cabin was unusual on a plantation where most slaves lived in communal slave quarters. But Betsey enjoyed more independence than other slaves, possibly because her husband, Isaac, was a free man. How he had obtained his freedom is uncertain, but an entry in Anthony's records listed him as "Isac Baley, free negrow."[2]

Frederick's memories of his early years were happy ones. Although he slept on straw and, for meals, scooped up corn mush with an oyster shell, he did not realize he was poor. And he

Grandmother Betsey

Betsey Bailey, Frederick Douglass's grandmother, was a skillful woman who brought many talents to the Lloyd plantation. She cared for children still too young for field work and served as a midwife. According to an 1809 record kept by Aaron Anthony, Betsey received about $2.40 for each baby she delivered.

Betsey was also skilled at fishing and made and sold large fishing nets called seines. Frederick recalled, "I have known her to be in the water waist deep, for hours, seine-hauling."[3] Her reputation as a gardener was widespread. Every year, people from all over asked her to plant their sweet potatoes. She knew just how far to place the seedlings in the ground—not too close to the surface and not too deep. "Superstition had it that her touch was needed to make them grow," Douglass wrote.[4] As a reward for a good crop, Betsey received part of the harvest.

Her knowledge about sweet potatoes may indicate that the Bailey family originated from a West Indies island, possibly Barbados. Sweet potatoes are indigenous to the West Indies. As early as the sixteenth century, African slaves were shipped to the West Indies to work on large sugar plantations. Many of those slaves were later sold in the mid-eighteenth century to American colonists.

did not know yet what it really meant to be a slave. He later described himself as "a spirited, joyous, uproarious, and happy boy, upon whom troubles fall only like water on a duck's back."[5] He played, he fished, he galloped like a horse, and he mimicked the roosters. But soon, his happy world was turned upside down.

The life-changing event happened to all the Bailey children. One by one, as they grew up, Betsey had to bring them to the Anthony cottage, by the main Lloyd plantation. From there, they would be put to work at an area farm. Perry, Sarah, and Eliza were already gone, and so were many of Frederick's cousins. Frederick had always known that his time would come, and he had dreaded that day.

One-Way Journey

In August 1824, Betsey told six-year-old Frederick they were going on a journey. She tied a fresh bandanna around her head and put cornbread in her pocket. Then, she took her grandson by the hand and headed southwest. They began a 12-mile (19-km) trek, a long walk for a young boy. From time to time, Betsey hoisted him on her shoulder to give him a rest.

At age six, Frederick was introduced to the realities of slavery at the Wye plantation in Easton, Maryland, shown here in modern times.

They came to the Wye House in Easton, where the Edward Lloyd family had lived since the 1780s. It was a large white mansion encircled by trees. The slaves referred to it as the Great House. The surrounding land included 13 farms, vast crops, and numerous slave quarters. There were blacksmith shops, carpenter shops, icehouses, greenhouses, and more. Nearby were elegant stables that housed some of the finest thoroughbred horses in the area.

Wye House Today

The Wye House in Talbot County, Maryland, still exists today and is owned and occupied by descendants of Edward Lloyd. In 1970, the U.S. government designated it worthy of preservation and listed it in the National Register of Historic Places.

The land had once produced tobacco but now was planted with wheat and corn. The plantation was one of the top wheat producers around.

Betsey and Frederick did not stop at the Great House, however. They kept walking to Aaron Anthony's brick cottage that overlooked the Wye River. Children were scurrying everywhere. Betsey pointed out to Frederick his brother Perry and sisters Sarah and Eliza. Then, she told him to go play with the children. Frederick went reluctantly, but he would not play. He stood fearfully and quietly by a wall while his grandmother stayed in the kitchen.

His Lot at Birth

It was not long before one of the children ran out of the kitchen and shouted, "Fed, Fed! grandmammy gone! grandmammy gone!"[6] In disbelief, Frederick rushed into the kitchen. His grandma was, indeed, gone. Heartbroken, he ran into the road, threw himself on the ground, and wept. Perry gave him a peach to make him feel better, but Frederick tossed it away. That night, he cried himself to sleep as resentment welled up inside him for the one person he had trusted most. He did not understand then that his grandmother had had no choice but to send him away, just as other slaves were. This was the lot he had been given at birth. He called the event his "first introduction to the realities of slavery."[7]

Frederick's new home was now the Anthony cottage. Fifty-four years would pass before he would return to the place where he had been born—the land where the log cabin nestled in the woods by the brook.

Songs of the Slave

Wherever there were slaves, there was usually singing. Frederick Douglass described their songs and the suffering behind them in his first autobiography: "They were tones loud, long, and deep; they breathed the prayer and complaint of souls boiling over with the bitterest anguish. Every tone was a testimony against slavery, and a prayer to God for deliverance from chains."[9]

More than a year later, in 1826, Frederick's mother died. He had seldom seen her since his move. However, on a few occasions, she had sneaked out at night and made the long walk to where Frederick lived. Sometimes, she would hold her son until he went to sleep and then walk back. She made sure she got back early in the morning before the slaves were called to the field. If she was late, she would be beaten severely. Frederick did not remember much about his mother. He would later say, "I received the tidings of her death with much the same emotions I should have probably felt at the death of a stranger."[8]

At Anthony cottage, Frederick had to get used to being a slave. He had to learn what it was like to be owned by a man he detested. He had to try to understand why he was forced to live a very different life from the white people at the Great House.

A slave mother grieves the forced separation from her child. Broken families were one of the harshest consequences of slavery.

Chapter 3

Whipping was a common punishment for slaves.

The Slave and the Whip

The Lloyds were one of the wealthiest families in Maryland. Edward Lloyd owned so many slaves that he divided them into groups and appointed overseers to manage them. In addition to being a slave owner himself, Aaron Anthony, known as Captain Anthony, supervised the overseers. Each overseer was responsible for a farm and the slaves who worked there.

The overseers made sure slaves worked hard and produced abundant crops. Some overseers were rude, others were harsh, and still others were outright cruel. The whip was used frequently on all slaves, whether young, old, male, or female. Typically, whippings were doled out to slaves who got up late for work.

Frederick had heard about the whippings, especially the story of a slave named Bill Demby. Austin Gore, who was Demby's overseer, had whipped the slave one day until blood streamed from his back. Demby ran into a nearby stream, dipping down to allow the water to soothe the slashes on his back. Then Gore came after him, calling to him three times to come out of the water. When Demby did not move, Gore raised his gun and shot him dead.

Aunt Hester's Punishment

Another gory whipping was witnessed by Frederick himself. It took place early one morning in Captain Anthony's kitchen, where the cries of a young woman woke Frederick from his sleep. Frederick slept on the floor of a small closet that opened into the kitchen. The cracks in the rough boards allowed him to see and hear what was going on without anyone noticing him. In the middle of the kitchen was Aunt Hester. She was hanging by her bound wrists from a strong hook in the ceiling, and her feet were on a bench. She had been stripped of her clothes from the waist up. Behind her stood Anthony with a whip in his hand.

Some 30 times or more, Anthony slashed Hester's back until it was bloody and raw. She screamed for mercy, but her pleas only infuriated Anthony more. Finally, he untied the injured girl and let her down. This was not the last time Anthony would punish Hester. Her crime was being in love with Ned Roberts, the handsome son of one of Colonel Lloyd's favorite slaves. Hester was a

No Justice for Austin Gore

Slave overseer Austin Gore was never brought to trial for killing the slave named Demby. Slaves were considered property only—not people. Killing a slave was not considered murder. If a person killed someone else's slave, he only needed to apologize to the owner and pay him what the slave was worth on the market.

beautiful young woman—Frederick called beauty a slave woman's curse—and perhaps Anthony wanted her for himself. But whatever the reason, Hester suffered greatly throughout her life at the hands of the overseer.

A Slave's Ration

Rules at the Wye plantation were strict for all slaves. They were told what to wear, what to eat, and what to do. Each slave had a yearly clothing allowance. An adult male received two shirts, two pairs of pants, one jacket, one pair of socks, and one pair of shoes. Children received only two shirts a year—long, rough linen shirts that hung to their knees. They had no other clothing, no socks, and no shoes. Frederick would later tell how common it was to see children during warm or cold weather "as destitute of clothing as any little heathen on the west coast of Africa. . . . [A]ll were nearly in a state of nudity."[1]

Adults received one blanket; the children got none. Everyone slept on the bare clay floors of the slave quarters. On chilly nights, the little ones curled up in holes or crannies to stay warm. Sometimes, they climbed into a corner of the large chimney and buried their feet in the warm ashes.

The overseer of each farm received a monthly allotment of food for his slaves. A slave's diet consisted usually of cornmeal, salt, and pickled pork or fish that was often tainted. Mealtimes were a crude experience. Frederick later wrote:

> *Our food was . . . put into a large wooden tray or trough, and set down upon the ground. The children were then called, like so many pigs, and like so many pigs they would come, and devour the mush; some with oyster-shells, others with pieces of shingle, some with naked hands, and none with spoons.*[2]

Aunt Katy, one of the slaves, was in charge of cooking and doling out food each day to the slaves. She was a cantankerous woman who showed no patience. She did not hesitate to smack the children with her hand or rebuke them with her sharp tongue. She was especially harsh with Frederick, whom she seemed to dislike more than the others. She often roughed him up or withheld his food. Frederick was usually hungry and constantly on the lookout for crumbs or leftovers he could steal.

Food was abundant on the Lloyd plantation, but slaves were not allowed to eat it. The lush garden with plenty of apples, oranges, and vegetables was off limits. To keep the slaves out, the fence around the

Slaves worked long hours growing crops for plantation owners.

garden was coated with sticky tar. If slaves were caught with tar on their clothes, they were severely beaten.

The Master's Son

Since Frederick was still too young to work in the fields, he helped around the Anthony house, brought the cows in at night, and kept the birds out of the garden. He was also told to spend time with Daniel, the Lloyds' youngest son. Frederick was Daniel's playmate as well as his servant. When the boys played in the Lloyd mansion, Frederick asked endless questions about this world of wealth and adult activities that intrigued his curious mind. When Daniel went hunting, Frederick went along to retrieve the birds Daniel shot. Their friendship blossomed, with a lack of prejudice that often comes naturally to children. Daniel also became a sort of protector to Frederick, keeping the other boys from bullying him.

Lloyd Politicians

Edward Lloyd V, owner of the Wye House, was governor of Maryland from 1809 to 1811. Between 1819 and 1826, when Douglass lived on the plantation, Lloyd was a U.S. senator. His grandson, Henry Lloyd, later became Maryland's fortieth governor, from 1885 to 1888. Henry Lloyd was the son of Daniel Lloyd, Douglass's playmate as a child.

Lucretia

Frederick also found favor with Anthony's daughter, Lucretia, who lived in her father's house with her new husband, Thomas Auld. Lucretia took a liking to Frederick and provided him favors, extra food, and sympathy when he needed it most.

She protected him from Aunt Katy's anger and mistreatment whenever possible.

In 1826, when Frederick was eight, circumstances changed at the Lloyd plantation. Aaron Anthony lost his position as plantation manager. He packed up his family and slaves and moved to another farm. But Lucretia and Thomas Auld made other arrangements for Frederick. They arranged for him to travel across the Chesapeake Bay and live in Baltimore with Thomas's brother, Hugh Auld, and his wife, Sophia. The Aulds in Baltimore said they needed

Escape Is Possible

On August 27, 1825, about seven months before Frederick Bailey set sail for Baltimore, two of Frederick's relatives—Aunt Jenny and Uncle Noah—escaped from the Lloyd plantation. Rumor had it that Aaron Anthony was going to sell them to an Alabama slave trader who planned to take them South. Anthony offered a reward of $100 for the return of Noah and $50 for Jenny. His advertisement read in part:

> *Ran away from the Subscriber, . . . negro man Noah, 26 years old, about 5 feet 10 or 11 inches high, stout and black, has very full ill shaped feet and is clumsy in his walk; negro Jenny, 26 years old, of a chestnut colour, middling size, and a well shaped woman.*[3]

The couple was never found, and Anthony ended up selling their two small children, ages six and seven, to a slave trader. Talk among the slaves filtered down to Frederick, who for the first time realized a slave could escape and live free. The thought never left him that one day he, too, might escape from slavery. "Young as I was," he later wrote, "I was already, in spirit and purpose, a fugitive from slavery."[4]

help raising their two-year-old son, Tommy. However, the move was most likely Lucretia's attempt to give Frederick a better life.

Remembering

Frederick Douglass's memory and attention to detail were remarkable. He once wrote, "Memory was given to man for some wise purpose. The past is . . . the mirror in which we may discern the dim outlines of the future and by which we may make them more symmetrical."[5]

Lucretia told Frederick he was leaving for Baltimore in three days. But first, he had to get rid of what she called the "scurf" of the plantation. Frederick willingly went to the creek every day and scrubbed himself. Layers of dirt came off his body, and dead skin fell from his calloused knees and cracked feet. When Frederick presented himself to Lucretia, she approved and dressed him in a nice shirt and pair of trousers. It was the first pair of pants he had ever worn.

On a Saturday morning in March 1826, Frederick boarded the *Sally Lloyd* and set sail for Baltimore. The voyage across the Chesapeake Bay to Maryland's mainland would change his life forever.

Frederick Douglass as a young man

Chapter 4

Baltimore was a bustling center for shipbuilding and trade in the mid-nineteenth century.

Baltimore

The *Sally Lloyd* was packed with sheep the day eight-year-old Frederick Bailey sailed to Baltimore. When the ship docked at Smith's Wharf, Frederick helped herd the sheep up the hill to the slaughterhouse. Then Tom, a deckhand and

Frederick's cousin, walked Frederick to his new home in the Fells Point district on the corner of Aliceanna Street and Happy Alley.

The sights along the way amazed Frederick. Houses stood close to one another, and horse-drawn carriages filled with well-dressed people clattered down the cobblestone street. People—blacks and whites alike—walked with a confidence and freedom that Frederick had never seen before.

Meeting the Aulds

At the Auld home, Tom knocked on the door. When it opened, Frederick immediately saw the kind, smiling face of Sophia Auld. Next to "Miss Sopha," as he would call her, was her husband, Hugh Auld. Peeking out from behind Sophia's skirt was two-year-old Tommy.

Life with the Hugh Auld family was very different from anything Frederick had ever experienced. He felt special, not just one of dozens of tattered little children scampering about on a farm. He now wore pants and a shirt, slept on a nice straw mattress with a warm woolen blanket, and ate good food until he was full. He felt like a real member of the family. He quickly came to adore Sophia, who treated him with extreme kindness and gentleness. She reminded him of Lucretia, his friend and protector at the plantation.

Baltimore Shipyards

After a few days, Frederick ventured out of the house and explored the neighborhood. Fells Point was a shipbuilding district where the world-famous Baltimore clippers were built. Nearly everyone worked at the shipyards or wharves, where goods flowed in and out of the busy harbor. Hugh Auld worked at a shipyard where a 64-gun warship was being built. It was the largest ship yet to come out of Baltimore. The ship launched just weeks after Frederick's arrival.

The noise of voices awoke Frederick at dawn on May 11, 1826. More than half the population of Baltimore was headed to the harbor to witness the launch. At approximately 10:30 a.m., some 40,000 people watched as the ship moved gracefully out to sea. The crowd shouted and cheered.

Baltimore Clippers

Baltimore was known for the Baltimore clipper, a small, swift-sailing ship developed in the eighteenth century. Its speed made it ideal for carrying perishables such as tea from China. In 1851, the *Flying Cloud* set a record. It traveled from New York City to San Francisco, sailing south all the way around the tip of South America, in just 89 days. Clippers were also used to transport slaves.

A military band played, families ate lunch on the grass, and shipyard workers drank rum and brandy. It was a celebration Frederick would never forget.

Sophia

By summer, Frederick was getting used to his pleasant new surroundings. He sometimes missed family members on the other side of the Chesapeake Bay, but he had no desire to return there. Being part of a white family was a new experience for Frederick. And having a slave in her home was a new experience for Sophia. Frederick was often overwhelmed by the goodness shown by Sophia, "a woman of the kindest heart and finest feelings."[1] Frederick knew that her love for him was special—love as deep as a mother for a son.

Sophia was often troubled by Frederick's fear and uncertainties. She had to encourage him not to act like a slave. When his voice trembled with fear, she built up his confidence. Slaves were never allowed to look their masters in the eye, and sometimes Frederick refused to let his eyes meet Sophia's. But she encouraged him to meet her gaze. In turn, Hugh took it upon himself to remind Sophia that Frederick was, indeed, still a slave.

Frederick had been in Baltimore more than a year when he was clearly reminded of his official status. His legal owner, Aaron Anthony, had died in November 1826. According to law, Anthony's property—and slaves were considered property—would be divided equally among his three children—Andrew, Richard, and Lucretia. But in the summer of 1827, Lucretia also died. Now her portion of the inheritance would go to her husband, Thomas Auld.

Back to the Eastern Shore

In early October 1827, Hugh Auld received word in Baltimore that Frederick had to return to the Anthony cottage on the Eastern Shore near Tuckahoe Creek. Anthony's slaves and his other property would be valued and

Path to Freedom

February is now Black History Month. That month was chosen to include the birthdays of two important people in black history: Frederick Douglass and Abraham Lincoln.

During the month, Baltimore boasts several events that highlight its black history. One of them is the Frederick Douglass "Path to Freedom" Walking Tour, which winds through the historic Fells Point district. It includes markers that indicate where Douglass lived, learned to read, and worked at the shipyards. Memorials to Douglass include a marker in Fells Point Square and a statue at Morgan State University. Also in the city are five houses called Douglass Place, which Douglass had built on Strawberry Alley when he was in his seventies. The houses still stand today, although the street has been renamed Dallas Street.

distributed among his heirs. Sophia sobbed and held Frederick close while he, too, wept bitterly. Frederick later recalled that difficult day: "The probabilities of ever seeing [Sophia] again, trembling in the balance as they did, could not be viewed without alarm and agony."[2]

Nine-year-old Frederick boarded a slow schooner and headed east across the Chesapeake Bay. Memories filled Frederick's head when he arrived back at the Anthony cottage, down the path from the huge Lloyd mansion. There, he joined 28 other slaves, including cruel-hearted Aunt Katy and beautiful Aunt Hester. His siblings were also there: Perry, 15; Sarah, 13; Eliza, 11; Kitty, 7; and Arianna, 5. Frederick's emotions ran deep when he saw his grandmother, Betsey. He had not seen her since his fateful journey with her to the Anthony farm.

Frederick did not fit in anymore with these slaves. He was dressed in nice clothes, and he talked like the people in Baltimore. But legally, he was still a slave. On October 18, 1827, Frederick and his family lined up to be evaluated by two property appraisers. The slaves would be assessed along with a number of pigs, sheep, cattle, and horses. Each piece of property—human, animal, or object—was given a dollar value.

The scene that unfolded made a deep impression on young Frederick:

> *What an assemblage! . . . Horses and men—cattle and women—pigs and children—all holding the same rank in the scale of social existence; and all subjected to the same narrow inspection, to ascertain their value in gold and silver—the only standard of worth applied by slaveholders to slaves!*[3]

The slaves were divided into three groups of approximately equal value. Each of Aaron Anthony's children received a group of slaves. Frederick hoped he was not in Andrew's group. Recently, he had seen Andrew brutally attack his brother, Perry. Andrew had grabbed Perry by the throat, thrown him to the ground, and stomped on his head with the heel of his boot. Frederick would not forget the gruesome sight of Perry's blood gushing from his nose and ear.

As chance would have it, Frederick ended up in the group that went with the recently deceased Lucretia's husband, Thomas Auld. Almost immediately, Thomas sent Frederick back to Baltimore, back to Hugh and Sophia Auld and little Tommy. For the next five and a half years, Frederick would once again live in Maryland's urban center.

At slave auctions, blacks were put on display and appraised by buyers.

Chapter 5

Abolitionist newspaper editor William Lloyd Garrison was an inspiration to young Frederick.

Motivated to Learn

In Baltimore, Frederick's life was fairly free of prejudice. The Aulds had moved to a house on Philpot Street, where the young neighborhood children did not care if Frederick's skin was darker than theirs. But Frederick made sure he avoided some of the older boys who sometimes teased and insulted him.

At home, Sophia treated him like her own son, and Tommy was just like a brother. Sophia was a religious woman, a Methodist who believed slavery went against the very laws of God. She sang hymns around the house and devoted herself to regular Bible reading. Often, she put Tommy on one knee and the Bible on the other and read out loud. She encouraged Frederick to stand by her side and listen. Frederick was fascinated with what he called the "mystery of reading."[1] Before long, he mustered up enough courage to ask Miss Sopha to teach him to read:

> *I frankly asked her to teach me to read; and, without hesitation, the dear woman began the task, and very soon, by her assistance, I was master of the alphabet, and could spell words of three or four letters.*[2]

Sophia enthusiastically shared Frederick's progress with everyone. She announced that she would continue teaching him until he could at least read the Bible.

However, her husband was not pleased. Hugh explained to his wife the true nature of slavery and

Link to the Midwest

In 1828, construction of the Baltimore & Ohio (B&O) Railroad began. It linked Baltimore with midwestern markets and turned the city into a major manufacturing center.

the rules that owners had to follow. One of those rules was that masters did not teach their slaves to read. In fact, it was against the law. He forbade Sophia to teach Frederick anymore. He warned her that if Frederick learned how to read, "it would forever unfit him for the duties of a slave." Knowledge would do him "a great deal of harm—making him disconsolate and unhappy."[3]

Knowledge and Reading

Frederick heard Hugh's harsh words. "[They] sunk deep into my heart," he wrote, "and stirred up not only my feelings into a sort of rebellion, but awakened within me a slumbering train of vital thought." If the ability to read was "the direct pathway from slavery to freedom," then he would certainly acquire it.[4]

In the years that followed, Frederick took every opportunity to learn how to read. He convinced the poor white children in the neighborhood to teach him what they knew. In return, he gave them delicious white bread from Sophia's kitchen.

When little Tommy started school, Frederick went to work at the shipyard. He asked the other workers about letters that were scrawled on ships during construction. At night, by candlelight in his attic room, he copied letters from an old Webster's speller in his house. He also found some of Tommy's old writing books that Sophia had stored in the kitchen; he devoured their contents. When Frederick went on errands, he tucked a book under his clothes and read as much of it as he could before he returned home.

Abolition and Emancipation

Eventually, Frederick mustered enough courage to walk into a bookstore and buy a book with 50 cents of his own hard-earned money. The book, a collection of speeches, was called *The Columbian Orator*. His favorites were the speeches that focused on slavery, abolition, and emancipation. Frederick was also keenly aware of what people in Baltimore were saying about slavery and the slave trade. He took particular notice of the words of Benjamin Lundy, the founder of the Baltimore antislavery newspaper, *Genius of Universal Emancipation*.

In 1830, Frederick heard about William Lloyd Garrison, editor of a Vermont newspaper. Garrison

William Lloyd Garrison

William Lloyd Garrison, celebrated abolitionist, continually called for the immediate emancipation of slaves in the United States. In 1831, he began publishing the *Liberator*, a radical antislavery newspaper. In 1833, he started the American Anti-Slavery Society, which grew to 250,000 members in its first five years.

had come to Baltimore to be co-editor of Lundy's newspaper. The newspaper targeted slave traders and shipowners who regularly shipped slaves to Southern states such as Mississippi, where the horrors of slavery were the worst. The shipowners sued Garrison, who ended up with a fine and jail time. But Garrison seemed energized by the turn of events.

On January 1, 1831, Garrison published the first issue of his new newspaper, the *Liberator.* His goal was to abolish slavery through the power of the printed word. He proclaimed in his paper, "AND I WILL BE HEARD."[5]

Resolved to Run Away

Frederick continued to learn more and more about abolition and the antislavery movement. He read whatever he could and talked to people on the streets. One day on the wharf, he helped two Irishmen unload their cargo. One of them asked Frederick if he was a slave. Frederick admitted that he was. Deeply concerned by Frederick's statement, one Irishman said it was a pity that a fine fellow like him should be a slave for life. Frederick soon picked up on both men's deep hatred for slavery. They even encouraged Frederick to receive help from the Underground Railroad and run away to the North. Frederick would eventually discover that this "railroad" was actually a network of people who helped slaves escape to free Northern states and Canada.

Frederick was not sure he could trust these men, however.

First Issue of the *Liberator*

On January 1, 1831, William Lloyd Garrison published the first issue of the *Liberator*. One of his first articles read in part:

> *I determined, at every hazard, to lift up the standard of emancipation in the eyes of the nation. . . . That standard is now unfurled; and long may it float, unhurt by the spoliations of time or the missiles of a desperate foe—yea, till every chain be broken, and every bondman set free! Let southern oppressors tremble—let their secret abettors tremble—let their northern apologists tremble—let all the enemies of the persecuted blacks tremble. . . .*
>
> *Assenting to the "self-evident truth" maintained in the American Declaration of Independence, "that all men are created equal, and endowed by their Creator with certain inalienable rights—among which are life, liberty and the pursuit of happiness," I shall strenuously contend for the immediate enfranchisement of our slave population. . . .*
>
> *I am in earnest—I will not equivocate—I will not excuse—I will not retreat a single inch—AND I WILL BE HEARD. The apathy of the people is enough to make every statue leap from its pedestal, and to hasten the resurrection of the dead.* [6]

White men often persuaded slaves to escape and then captured them and returned them to their owners for a reward. Frederick ended the conversation, but he did not stop thinking about what the men had said. "I nevertheless remembered their advice," he wrote, "and from that time I resolved to run away. I looked forward to a time at which it would be safe for me to escape."[7]

What happened in 1833, however, halted Frederick's plans. Once again, he was sent back to his owner, Thomas Auld. No one is sure why he had to leave Baltimore. Perhaps word got back to Hugh Auld that Frederick was getting involved in the antislavery movement. Or perhaps rumors of an escape plan leaked out. No matter the reason, Frederick had no choice but to return to his master. Thomas had remarried, to a woman named Rowena Hamilton. They now lived in St. Michaels, on the peninsula, west of Tuckahoe.

In March 1833, 15-year-old Frederick boarded a boat, the *Amanda*, and sailed to the port at St. Michaels. What lay ahead would be the cruelest and most challenging time of his life.

$200 Reward.

Ranaway from the subscriber, last night, a mulatto man named **FRANK MULLEN**, about twenty-one years old, five feet ten or eleven *9 or 10* inches high. He wears his hair long at the sides and top, close behind, and keeps it nicely combed; rather thick lips, mild countenance, polite when spoken to, and very genteel in his person. His clothing consists of a variety of summer and winter articles, among which are a blue cloth coat and blue casinet coatee, white pantaloons, blue cloth do., and a pair of new ribbed casinet do., a blue Boston wrapper, with velvet collar, several black hats, boots, shoes, &c. As he has absconded without any provocation, it is presumed he will make for Pennsylvania or New-York. I will give one hundred dollars if taken in the State of Maryland, or the above reward if taken any where east of that State, and secured so that I get him again, and all reasonable expenses paid if brought home to the subscriber, living in the city of Washington.

THOS. C. SCOTT.

October **21, 1835.**

P.S. I will give the above reward of $200 if taken out of the District of Columbia

Nov 25. 1835 *Thos C Scott*

Offering monetary rewards was one way slave owners pursued runaway slaves.

Chapter 6

NARRATIVE

OF THE

LIFE

OF

FREDERICK DOUGLASS,

AN

AMERICAN SLAVE.

WRITTEN BY HIMSELF.

BOSTON:
PUBLISHED AT THE ANTI-SLAVERY OFFICE,
No. 25 CORNHILL
1845.

Douglass vividly recounted his years as a slave in his 1845 autobiography, Narrative of the Life of Frederick Douglass, an American Slave.

Return to Slavery

Living virtually as a free person for seven years in Baltimore made Frederick's 1833 return to slavery an especially bitter experience. At the home of Thomas and Rowena Auld, Frederick reunited with his relatives. His disfigured cousin,

Henny, was there. She had been burned so badly as a child that her body was deformed and her hands closed shut. So frustrated was Thomas with her disabilities that he repeatedly whipped her.

Frederick's sister Eliza was also there. She had learned a sort of silent rebellion against her master. At times she just happened to forget what she was supposed to do or lost a tool here and there. She worked at about half her capacity. Other slaves quietly rebelled in the same way. It was not long before Frederick was following their example.

Eliza Bailey

Eliza Bailey, Frederick Douglass's older sister, lived to be 60 years old. Records indicate that Aaron Anthony, her mother's white owner, was her biological father.

Edward Covey, Slave Breaker

In January 1834, about ten months after Frederick arrived, Thomas Auld was fed up with his rebellion and sent him to work for Edward Covey, the slave breaker. Covey could turn a rebellious slave into a hardworking, profitable worker. Frederick's first punishment from Covey occurred after his trip to the woods to gather firewood in the ox-drawn cart. Forced to go back into the forest, Frederick received the first whipping of his life. But it was only the first of countless incidents where Covey would nab an opportunity to catch Frederick by surprise and punish him. The slaves called Covey "the snake" for his ability to "coil up" in the grass and pounce unexpectedly on his victims. He seemed to be hiding behind every bush and tree.

Once, when Frederick collapsed on a hot summer day, Covey seemed to appear from nowhere. He kicked Frederick again and again, and then gashed his head with a piece of wood. With blood pouring from his

Hypocrisy

Frederick Douglass once had a meaningful religious conversion experience. But later, he became fed up with the hypocrisy in churches where blacks had to sit in special places. He also condemned white slaveholders who claimed to be Christian men but owned slaves and abused them. He was particularly outraged with his owner, Thomas Auld, who claimed he had a religious conversion at a Methodist camp meeting. Frederick hoped it would mean better treatment for the slaves, but he was wrong. Auld continued to treat them with the same cruelty and unkindness as he had before. And now he justified it on religious grounds.

Auld was especially brutal to Frederick's disfigured cousin Henny. Frederick wrote how Auld would "tie up this lame and maimed woman and whip her in a manner most brutal and shocking; and then with blood-chilling blasphemy he would quote the passage of scripture, 'That servant which knew his lord's will and prepared not himself, neither did according to his will, shall be beaten with many stripes.'"[1]

head, Frederick ran through the woods, all the way back to Thomas Auld's house, for help. When he arrived, Auld offered neither help nor sympathy and sent him back to Covey the next morning.

Turning Point

On his way back, Frederick happened upon Sandy Jenkins, a slave on his way to a cabin nearby to visit his wife, a free woman. Frederick stayed the night there and then quietly wandered back into Covey's barn on Monday morning. At first Covey ignored his runaway slave. But then he tried to grab Frederick's feet and tie them together. Frederick pounced on his master, no longer afraid. Covey was shocked by Frederick's retaliation. As the two wrestled, Frederick grabbed Covey's throat and drew blood. Then the fight continued outside. Covey's attempts to get other slaves to help him proved futile.

The men fought for two hours, rolling and tumbling on the ground and throwing each other down at every opportunity. When the fight ended, Covey claimed victory. But Frederick had gotten the best of his slave breaker. Covey never touched Frederick again. Frederick would call the event a turning point in his life:

I was a changed being after that fight. I was nothing before; I WAS A MAN NOW. It . . . inspired me with a renewed determination to be a FREEMAN.[2]

The Mysterious Herb

When Douglass defeated Covey in a two-hour scuffle, he gave some of the credit to a mysterious herb. Fellow slave Sandy Jenkins had given him the herb, claiming it had the power to protect him. If Douglass wore the herb on his right side, he claimed, no white man would ever strike him or whip him. Douglass was never sure if the herb had those powers or if wearing it merely gave him added confidence.

The Freeland Farm

On Christmas Day that year, Frederick's one-year obligation to Covey ended, and he headed back to Thomas Auld. Almost immediately, he was rented out to William Freeland. The Freeland farm was about three miles (4.8 km) from St. Michaels. It overlooked the beautiful Chesapeake Bay, which rekindled Frederick's desire for freedom.

Frederick made good friends at the Freeland farm with a group of intelligent young men, but only Frederick could read. Before long, Frederick organized a sort of school that met on Sundays under a large oak tree. When the weather turned cold, the group met at the home of a free black man, whose name and location were never disclosed. Frederick had smuggled the old Webster's speller and *The Columbian Orator* to the farm. Now, he used them to teach as many as 30 slaves how to read.

Escape Plan

Soon, Frederick and five of his students were planning their escape. The students were John and Henry Harris, Henry Bailey, Sandy Jenkins, and Charles Roberts.

Their plan was to steal a large canoe and head up the Chesapeake Bay along the uneven peninsula shore. At the north point of the peninsula, they would slip away on foot to Pennsylvania, a free state. Since Frederick knew how to write, he created fake passes—permission from their master to travel. At the last minute, Sandy Jenkins backed out of the plot. Now there were five.

The Freeland Farm

William Freeland was not like most of the slave owners for whom Frederick Douglass worked. Douglass described him as open, mild, and frank—a well-bred Southern gentleman. At the Freeland farm, the slaves were fed well and given plenty of time to eat their meals. Work ended at sundown, when slaves had time for themselves.

Fugitive slaves crossing a river in Rappahannock County, Virginia, 1862

On Saturday morning, April 2, 1836, Frederick felt something was wrong. The horn sounded for breakfast, and Frederick and John Harris walked toward the house. Down the long path they saw four horses with white riders. Tied behind were Henry Bailey and Charles Roberts. They had been whipped and dragged down the road. Frederick knew it was all over. Someone had betrayed them.

Dragged through the Streets

In the kitchen, Frederick and John Harris were seized. Freeland ordered them to go outside. Their white captors bound their hands behind their backs. Henry Harris resisted fiercely, putting up a good fight before all four white men cocked their pistols and aimed them at his head. "Shoot me, shoot me!" Henry said. "You can't kill me but once. Shoot, shoot,—and be damned! I *won't be tied!*"[3] In the end, Henry was subdued.

Frederick recalled, "We were to be dragged that morning fifteen miles behind horses, and then to be placed in the Easton jail."[4] Before they left, Freeland's mother brought out some fresh biscuits for John and Henry to take with them. During Henry Harris's struggle, Frederick had managed to throw his fake pass into the fire. He now whispered to Henry and John to put their passes inside the biscuits. Frederick told them to eat the biscuits as well as the passes. Tangible evidence of their attempted escape would be gone.

While townspeople looked on, Frederick and the four others who had wished to escape with him were dragged through town. Almost immediately, slave traders showed up to look over the five slaves.

They taunted them and examined them to estimate what price these strong black men might bring in the Southern slave market. But the slave traders did not get their chance to buy these men. Two days later, Freeland took four of them home. He left Frederick to languish in jail alone for another week.

When Freeland eventually retrieved Frederick, he announced that the young slave was going to be sold to a friend in Alabama. However, Thomas Auld had other plans. A few days later, he put Frederick on a boat and sent him back to Baltimore—once again to live with Hugh Auld. "My master sent me away, because there existed against me a very great prejudice in the community, and he feared I might be killed," Frederick later wrote, explaining his master's decision.[5] Thomas promised Frederick that if he behaved himself, he would be a free man at the age of 25.

At the Freeland farm, Douglass rose as a leader. His ability to inspire others would make him one of the most successful abolitionists of his day.

Chapter 7

During his escape, Douglass traveled from Baltimore to New Bedford, Massachusetts, stopping in cities along the way.

Escape to New York

Frederick Bailey was a different person when he returned to Baltimore in 1836. He was 18, physically strong, and a tough survivor of abuse and humiliation. He again lived with the Hugh Auld family, who had moved to a house on Fells

Street. Tommy, now a teenager, showed little interest in continuing their childhood friendship, which had been free of racial barriers. Frederick recalled, "In childhood, he scarcely considered me inferior to himself—certainly, as good as any other boy with whom he played; but the time had come when his *friend* must become his *slave*."[1]

Shunned

Frederick's old neighborhood friends also shunned him, as did Sophia. She had kept her distance ever since her husband had reproached her for teaching Frederick to read. Hugh had not changed; he saw himself only as a master. Right away, he arranged for Frederick to work as an apprentice at William Gardner's shipyard. Since Frederick was still a slave, he turned over his wages to Auld.

Baltimore had also changed. Thousands of immigrants from poverty-stricken Ireland had flooded the city and taken any jobs they could—jobs previously held by blacks. The number of free blacks in the city had also grown. Job competition was fierce, and racial tensions ran high. At Gardner's shipyard, the Irish refused to work until Gardner fired the black apprentices.

Frederick helped build slave ships used for bringing Africans to North America.

Gardner gave in and fired all of them except Frederick, who was assigned to work with four white apprentices. They worked together on the deck of a warship being built for the U.S. government. The white men made life unbearable for Frederick. They cursed him, baited him, and attacked him with tools and axes. But Frederick fought back, no doubt emboldened by the victory he had once had over Covey.

Attacked

After work one evening, Frederick's tormentors waited for him in the shadows outside the shipyard's gate. The men kicked and beat him viciously with bricks, metal spikes, and fists. A crowd of approximately 50 white workers gathered, shouting, "Kill him! Kill him . . . knock his brains out."[2] Somehow, Frederick was able to slip away and run home.

At the sight of Frederick's bloody eye and battered face, Sophia cried. She cleaned him up and, to soothe his badly injured eye, she placed a piece of raw meat on it. Hugh Auld was furious that his slave had been attacked and demanded a warrant for the arrest of Frederick's assailants. But according to Maryland law, nothing could be done unless a witness—one of the white workers—came forward. When none of them would testify, Auld gave up.

Auld now arranged a job for Frederick at the Walter Price shipyard, where he himself worked. Ironically, Frederick began working on ships—the *Delorez*, the *Teayer*, and the *Eagle*—meant to transport slaves. They were designed to outrun British warships that were trying to block slave traffic out of West Africa.

Friendships and Freedom Talk

Frederick struck up some good friendships at the shipyard. His five closest friends were free blacks with similar interests—reading, talking, and debating about Maryland's black population and free states in the North. Frederick's friends belonged to a debate group called the East Baltimore Mental Improvement Society. Before long, Frederick joined the club. The members met secretly to discuss some of the most controversial subjects of the time, especially slavery. They also

Blocking Slave Trade

In 1808, an act of Congress outlawed the importation of slaves into the United States. However, slave traders figured out ways to smuggle slaves into the country. Great Britain was actively trying to stop illegal African slave trade by blockading the West African coast with warships. Slave ships could only avoid the blockade by outrunning the British vessels. Thus the need arose for newer, swifter slave ships. The narrow, fast-sailing Baltimore clippers were the perfect solution.

The Walter Price shipyard in Baltimore was one of the main suppliers of swift clippers in the early nineteenth century. Although the purpose of the ships was a secret, it was common knowledge on the docks that they were built for the slave trade.

In 1820, a U.S. law made shipbuilding for the slave trade an act of piracy punishable by death. Price and other shipbuilders skirted the law with a complex scheme. New ships were routed to Liverpool, England, where they were outfitted for transporting slaves. Since the ships flew the U.S. flag, the British could not stop them. In Africa, the ship was loaded with slaves, and the flag was switched to another country's.

read articles and speeches by abolitionists such as William Lloyd Garrison, Theodore Weld, Benjamin Lundy, and Lewis Tappan. They encouraged one another with the antislavery speeches that U.S. Representative John Quincy Adams of Massachusetts was presenting to Congress.

Anna Murray

At a meeting in 1837, Frederick met a free black woman named Anna Murray. She was a native of Maryland, born and raised just across Tuckahoe Creek from Frederick's birthplace. Shortly before her birth, her parents had been released from slavery, and thus she was born free. Although she could neither read nor write, she did play the violin, and she taught Frederick how to play. Anna and Frederick were attracted to each other, and their friendship grew into love. In 1838, they were engaged to be married.

Anna was concerned that Frederick was not a free man. Both of them were haunted by the fear that any day he could be "sold South"—bought by a slave trader and auctioned off in a Southern state. Encouraged by Anna, Frederick became even more determined to escape.

The Baltimore and Ohio Railroad now ran from Baltimore to Wilmington, Delaware. There, it connected to a steamboat line that made regular trips to Philadelphia, Pennsylvania. From there, a person could travel freely. Frederick decided to disguise himself as a sailor and take a one-way trip on the train and steamboat.

Fugitive in the North

For a while, Auld had allowed Frederick to keep part of his salary so that he could live on his own and buy his own food. But now, Auld was becoming suspicious of Frederick and ordered him to move back to the Auld household. Again, Frederick was required to turn over all his wages. Frederick now moved quickly. He borrowed "free papers" from a sailor friend. Free blacks carried these papers with them when they traveled to prove they were, indeed, free.

Dressed as a sailor in a red shirt, hat, and black neck scarf, Frederick boarded the train in Baltimore. He connected to the steamboat that took him to Philadelphia. That night, he traveled by train to New York. He later wrote:

My free life began on the third of September, 1838. On the morning of the 4th of that month, after an anxious and most perilous but safe journey, I found myself in the big city of New York, a free man. [3]

Frederick was not technically free. He was a runaway, and bounty hunters searched constantly for escaped slaves. For a price, they would return any slave to his or her master. But Frederick found safe refuge with David Ruggles, secretary of an abolitionist organization and member of the Underground Railroad.

Meanwhile, Frederick wrote to Anna, telling her of his safe arrival and asking her to join him. On September 15, 1838, Frederick Bailey and Anna Murray were married in New York City by the Reverend James W. C. Pennington, an African-American minister and abolitionist.

Having been warned that New York was not a safe place for runaways, Frederick and Anna traveled to New Bedford, Massachusetts. There, Mary and Nathan Johnson provided them a safe place to stay. At first, Frederick and

Abolitionist Preacher

The Reverend James W. C. Pennington, who married Frederick and Anna, was born a slave in Maryland. He eventually escaped to Pennsylvania and then to New York. In 1838, he finished his religious studies and became the minister of a black congregation.

Anna changed their surname to Johnson, after their kind hosts. But since Johnson was such a common name, Frederick asked Nathan to choose another name for them. Nathan chose Douglass, after the character in a book he was reading. Frederick Bailey—the slave—was now Frederick Douglass—the fugitive. But for the first time in his life, he truly felt like a free man.

Anna Murray's marriage to Frederick Douglass would last for more than four decades, until her death in 1882.

Chapter 8

Bronze statues commemorate the 1848 Women's Rights Convention, which Douglass attended with other feminists of his day.

Popular Orator

New Bedford, Massachusetts, on the northeast Atlantic coast, was a delightful place to live. Frederick Douglass was astonished by the city. "Everything looked clean, new, and beautiful," he wrote. "I was for once made glad by a view of extreme wealth, without being saddened by seeing extreme poverty."[1] Douglass was most impressed by how blacks were living:

> *I found many, who had not been seven years out of their chains, living in finer houses, and evidently enjoying more of the comforts of life, than the average of slaveholders in Maryland.*[2]

Douglass found a job working on ships at the wharf. But most important to him were the black friends he made there. He was amazed at their intelligence and lively conversations about issues that mattered most to him: slavery and liberty.

A Family

Frederick and Anna settled into the community and began establishing a family of their own. On June 24, 1839, their first child, Rosetta, was born. Sixteen months later, Lewis Henry came into the world.

The family attended church, first at a predominately white Methodist church, then at the African Methodist Episcopal Zion Church. The pastor, Thomas James, like Douglass, was a runaway slave and very involved in the antislavery movement.

Rosetta, the oldest Douglass child, grew up to preach the same truths as her father.

Douglass served in church leadership roles and sometimes preached. Once, he told the congregation what slavery was really like and why all slaves should be set free. News of his speech ended up in William Lloyd Garrison's newspaper, the *Liberator*.

Douglass called those New Bedford days some of the happiest of his life. But he longed for more. He was strongly influenced by Garrison. Wherever this slender, balding man with spectacles and a pointed nose traveled, he demanded the "immediate and complete emancipation of all slaves."[3] Douglass would never forget that message.

Rosetta Douglass

Rosetta, daughter of Frederick and Anna Douglass, became a public speaker like her father. She lectured alongside Sojourner Truth, the famous orator and abolitionist. Douglass married Nathan Sprague, a former slave, and together they had seven children. Many of their descendants still live in Rochester, New York.

Speaking Tours

In 1841, Douglass attended the summer convention of the Massachusetts Anti-Slavery Society on Nantucket Island, off the Massachusetts coast. Some of the most active abolitionists were there, including Garrison and William C. Coffin, who had once heard Douglass speak at the Zion Church. Coffin now asked him to speak at the convention. Hesitant, Douglass agreed. Since he was still a fugitive who could be captured and returned to his master, he did not share his entire story. But what he did say was so compelling that he was asked to travel around the country as a speaker for the society. Douglass accepted the offer.

That year, Frederick and Anna moved to Lynn, Massachusetts, to be closer to Boston, a center for abolitionists. Their family was also growing. In 1842, Frederick Jr. was born. Two years later, they had their fourth child, Charles. For almost four years, Douglass was rarely home. He traveled throughout the Northern states, speaking, lecturing, and debating about the evils of slavery.

As time went on, he became bolder and told more details of his life of slavery. In May 1845, he published his first autobiography, *Narrative of the Life of Frederick Douglass, an American Slave*. The book was extremely popular in the United States and Europe, with sales of about 5,000 in the first four months. But since he had identified his owner in the book, he was now forced into exile to avoid capture.

Safety in Great Britain

Douglass took refuge in the United Kingdom, where slavery had been illegal for 38 years. His first stop was Ireland. The people had heard many antislavery speeches, but they were particularly interested in Douglass's compelling story. His speeches brought standing-room-only crowds, and his popularity grew.

He began a speaking tour throughout Scotland and England. He encouraged and united abolitionists against slavery in the United States. His British friends were appalled that he was still legally a slave. They enthusiastically raised money to purchase his freedom. Soon, they presented Hugh Auld with $711.66, the price he had agreed on for the slave he knew as Frederick Bailey. Auld accepted the money, and Douglass was officially set free from slavery on December 5, 1846.

Freedom Papers

In 1846, Thomas Auld sold Douglass to Hugh Auld for $100. Douglass's friends then bought his freedom from Hugh Auld. In Douglass's freedom papers, Hugh Auld stated, "I, Hugh Auld, of the city of Baltimore, . . . have released from slavery, liberated, manumitted, and set free, . . . my negro man, named Frederick Baily, otherwise called Douglass."[4]

A Free Man

Now a free man, Douglass's self-confidence grew, as did his desire to spread the antislavery message. In 1847, he returned to the United States, where he started his own newspaper, the *North Star*, in Rochester, New York. Again, his British friends helped him by purchasing a printing press. The first issue was published on December 3, 1847.

Within two months, the newspaper was a remarkable success. In February 1848, Douglass moved his wife and four children to Rochester. The next year, Frederick and Anna had another child, a daughter named Annie.

Dump His Press in the Lake!

Not everyone was happy about Douglass's antislavery newspaper, which also supported women's suffrage, or right to vote. In fact, the *New York Herald* encouraged the citizens of Rochester to dump Douglass's printing press into Lake Ontario. But Rochester was also home to many strong abolitionists who supported

"This Fourth of July Is *Yours*, Not *Mine*"

In the 1850s, Douglass traveled extensively, speaking at a variety of events. On July 5, 1852, he gave one of his most emotional speeches, "The Meaning of July Fourth for the Negro." He was in Rochester, New York, at a commemoration of the signing of the Declaration of Independence. He began by honoring the memory of the signers of the Declaration. But then he asked his audience:

> *Fellow-citizens, pardon me, allow me to ask, why am I called upon to speak here to-day? What have I, or those I represent, to do with your national independence? . . .*
>
> *This Fourth of July is yours, not mine. You may rejoice, I must mourn. . . . My subject, then, fellow-citizens, is American slavery. I shall see this day and its popular characteristics from the slave's point of view. . . .*
>
> *What, to the American slave, is your 4th of July? I answer; a day that reveals to him, more than all other days in the year, the gross injustice and cruelty to which he is the constant victim. To him, your celebration is a sham; your boasted liberty, an unholy license; your national greatness, swelling vanity; your sounds of rejoicing are empty and heartless.*[5]

Douglass's cause. Leading female suffragists and abolitionists there included Susan B. Anthony, Lucretia Mott, and Elizabeth Cady Stanton.

In spite of the *North Star*'s popularity, it was not a moneymaker. After a year, Douglass returned to the speaking circuit to earn more money. Meanwhile, his British friend Julia Griffiths, who had helped launch the paper, rescued it from failure. In 1851, Douglass changed the name of his paper to *Frederick Douglass' Paper*. He was able to publish it weekly until 1860 and monthly through 1863.

John Brown

In 1848, Douglass had met an abolitionist who would alter the course of his life. His name was John Brown, a strong supporter of armed revolt as a way to end slavery. In 1857, Brown made plans to raid a weapons arsenal at Harpers Ferry, Virginia, and invade the South. There, he would arm slaves and help them rise up against their owners.

At first, Douglass had supported Brown's cause, when the abolitionist's plan was to use guerilla warfare to free slaves. But Douglass believed an attack on a federal weapons arsenal was too dangerous, and he backed out. On October 16, 1859, Brown and

21 other men raided Harpers Ferry. The following day, they were captured. Brown was found guilty of treason and hanged on December 2. When Brown was arrested, he had an old note from Douglass in his pocket. It was enough to link Douglass to the plot.

An arrest warrant went out for Douglass. However, he escaped to Canada and then sailed to England. He stayed there until news of the sudden death of his 11-year-old daughter, Annie, reached him. He was devastated at the loss of the daughter, who held a special place in his heart. Later, he wrote, "Deeply distressed by this bereavement, and acting upon the impulse of the moment, regardless of the peril, I at once resolved to return home."[6]

The events of the following year would rock the foundation of the United States. In 1860, the country's rift over slavery intensified. The United States was hurled into a civil war that would last four years.

THE NORTH STAR.

RIGHT IS OF NO SEX—TRUTH IS OF NO COLOR—GOD IS THE FATHER OF US ALL, AND ALL WE ARE BRETHREN.

I. NO. 31. ROCHESTER, N. Y., FRIDAY, JULY 28, 1848. WHOLE NO

Douglass published the North Star, *his abolitionist newspaper, from 1847 to 1851.*

Chapter 9

President Lincoln signed the Emancipation Proclamation in 1863. The act legally freed slaves, and it changed the tone of the Civil War.

War!

In May 1860, the Republican National Convention was held in Chicago, Illinois. Delegates waved banners that read, "No More Slave States." Frederick Douglass would have preferred "Death to Slavery." By the end of the convention, however, a man who hated slavery—Abraham Lincoln—was nominated as the Republican presidential candidate.

Lincoln and Civil War

Southerners opposed Lincoln, afraid he would put an end to slavery completely. Douglass was afraid he would not. After all, Lincoln had stated his view clearly in several speeches. In an 1859 debate in Cincinnati, Ohio, he had said:

> *I say that we must not interfere with the institution of slavery in the States where it exists, because the Constitution forbids it, and the general welfare does not require us to do so.*[1]

Lincoln easily won the election. By the time he was inaugurated on March 4, 1861, seven Southern states had seceded. Four more followed over the next three months. Those 11 states formed their own country, the Confederate States of America.

At 4:00 a.m. on April 12, 1861, the Confederates opened fire on Fort Sumter, a U.S. military post in North Carolina. The Civil War had begun. Douglass said, "For this consummation we have watched and wished with fear and trembling. God be praised! that it has come at last."[2]

Douglass worked tirelessly in the war effort, giving speeches, writing articles, and urging President Lincoln to issue a proclamation freeing all slaves. He also pressed Lincoln to allow thousands of willing young black men to enlist in the Union army.

The Emancipation Proclamation

On January 1, 1863, President Lincoln issued his Emancipation Proclamation. Part of it read that "all persons held as slaves within any State or designated part of a State, the people whereof shall then be in rebellion against the United States, shall be then, thenceforward, and forever free."[3] Four million slaves in the South were now legally free.

Political compromises kept Lincoln from declaring emancipation for all slaves. The proclamation ended slavery only in states not under Union control. Slave states loyal to the Union, such as Maryland, were allowed to continue the practice, as Lincoln did not want to risk losing their support.

Letter from Perry

In 1867, Frederick Douglass received a letter from his brother, Perry, who was finally a free man. Now he was eager to move North with his wife and children. Douglass arranged for them to come to Rochester, New York, and had a house built for them on his land. He wrote, "The meeting with my brother after nearly forty years separation is an event altogether too affecting to describe."[4]

A memorial in Boston, Massachusetts, honors black soldiers of the 54th Massachusetts Regiment, one of the first black units in the U.S. military.

The proclamation was a crucial development in the Civil War. It symbolized victory for U.S. blacks everywhere, even if it could not be enforced until the South was defeated. It also raised the stakes of the conflict. From this point on, the issue of slavery was intimately tied to the Civil War. And the Emancipation Proclamation had an important practical result: it allowed black men to fill the depleted ranks of the Union army.

"Men of Color, to Arms"

Douglass was ecstatic. Most black men were now free, and they could serve in all branches of the military. Douglass began traveling all over the North, recruiting black men for the Union army in the newly formed all-black unit, the Fifty-fourth Massachusetts Volunteer Infantry Regiment. The March 1863 issue of *Douglass' Monthly* announced, "Men of Color, to Arms."[5] The first recruit to sign up was Douglass's own son Charles. Douglass's son Lewis also enlisted shortly thereafter.

By the spring of 1863, about 1,000 black men in the

The Fifty-fourth Massachusetts Infantry

The Fifty-fourth Massachusetts Volunteer Infantry Regiment, one of the first black units in the U.S. military, fought extensively in the Civil War. The soldiers trained at Camp Meigs near Boston and left to fight in the war in May 1863. Although their first duties were manual labor, they were called into battle in South Carolina in July.

The soldiers were promised pay equal to white soldiers, but at first they did not receive it. A black soldier received $7 a month; a white soldier was paid $13. In 1864, while the war was going on, Congress passed a bill that guaranteed equal pay for black troops. The soldiers also received back pay to make up for having been underpaid since their service began.

The Fifty-fourth Infantry disbanded after the Civil War. A bronze monument honoring the unit was erected in Boston as part of the Black Heritage Trail. More than a century later, in 1989, the Fifty-fourth Infantry was featured in the Academy Award-winning film *Glory*. On November 21, 2008, the unit was reactivated as part of the Massachusetts National Guard to confer military honors at funerals and state functions.

Fifty-fourth Infantry were combat-ready. On May 28, Frederick Douglass met the regiment in Boston, where crowds cheered and waved as the men boarded a steamer that would take them to battle.

Assassination

In 1864, Lincoln won a second term as president. On April 9, 1865, Confederate General Robert E. Lee surrendered to Union General Ulysses S. Grant. The Civil War was over. Five days later, on April 14, John Wilkes Booth shot Lincoln at Ford's Theatre in Washington DC. Lincoln died the next morning.

Douglass was at home in Rochester when Lincoln died. At Rochester City Hall, mourners gathered to grieve the loss of the president who had freed Confederate slaves and won the Civil War. When Douglass entered the room, someone asked him to speak. He rose and said to his fellow Americans:

Refused Entry

In 1865, President Lincoln invited Douglass to his second inaugural reception. However, because Douglass was black, two policemen seized him at the door. Douglass bolted past but was stopped inside by two other officers. When Lincoln found out Douglass was there, he made sure his guest was allowed to enter.

I feel it as a personal as well as national calamity, on account of the race to which I belong and the deep interest which that good man ever took in its elevation. . . . Good man we call him; good man he was. [6]

Lincoln did not live to see the ratification of the Thirteenth Amendment on December 6, 1865. It declared, "Neither slavery nor involuntary servitude . . . shall exist within the United States."[7] It was truly the end of slavery—what Douglass had lived for and hoped for all his life.

Douglass considered giving up speaking and writing, resting in the bliss of freedom. But he soon discovered his next battle: the struggle for equal rights and improvement of the lives of black Americans. In the years that followed, Douglass would see a very slow progression toward equality under the law for blacks.

Lincoln's Walking Stick

In April 1865, Abraham Lincoln's funeral train carried his body through several states on the way to his home state of Illinois. When the train passed through New York City, black people, including Frederick Douglass, were not permitted to attend. In August, however, Mary Todd Lincoln, the assassinated president's wife, sent a gift to Douglass: her husband's favorite cane.

Department of the Interior,
Washington D. C. Augt. 10. 1863

To whom it may concern,

The bearer of this, Frederick Douglass, is known to us as a loyal free man, and is, hence, entitled to travel, unmolested,-

We trust he will be recognized everywhere, as a free man, and a gentleman.

Respectfully,
J. P. Usher
Secy.

S. C. Pomeroy
U. S. S
Kansas

I concur. A. Lincoln.
Aug. 10. 1863.

Pass the Bearer Fredrick Douglass who is known to me to be a free man M Blair

An 1863 letter signed by President Lincoln and three other officials documented that Frederick Douglass was a free man.

Douglass at his desk in his Washington DC home

Milestones

On July 9, 1868, former slaves became citizens of the United States with the passage of the Fourteenth Amendment. Nearly two years later, on February 3, 1870, black men were granted the freedom to vote. The Fifteenth

Amendment declared that the "right of citizens of the United States to vote shall not be denied or abridged by the United States or by any state on account of race, color, or previous condition of servitude."[1]

That month, another milestone in the struggle for equality occurred. Hiram Revels of Mississippi became the first black man elected to the U.S. Senate. Frederick Douglass's son Charles witnessed the swearing-in ceremony. Charles later admitted that he wished his father had been the one being sworn in that day.

Vice Presidential Candidate

Douglass, now in his fifties, turned his focus to politics. In 1872, he was nominated for vice president on the Equal Rights Party ticket. However, his party lost to the Republican ticket—Ulysses S. Grant and Henry Wilson. Douglass expected a post in Grant's administration, but he was not offered a position.

Douglass still spent much of his time working for equal rights.

Up in Flames

On June 2, 1872, Douglass's home burned to the ground. Arson was suspected. All family members got out of the house safely, and many books and much furniture were saved. However, Douglass's first issues of the *North Star* were destroyed along with many photographs and files.

He published a weekly newspaper, the *New National Era*, in which he hoped to inform white readers about equality. However, he had few white subscribers, and he stopped publishing the paper in 1874.

Cedar Hill

Douglass's last home, Cedar Hill, was given to the Frederick Douglass Memorial and Historical Association by Helen Pitts Douglass. The home was opened to visitors in 1916 and added to the National Park system in 1962. In 1988, it was designated a National Historic Site.

U.S. Marshal

From 1874 to 1877, Douglass served as president of the Freedman's Savings and Trust Company. In March 1877, he finally received a government appointment. Rutherford B. Hayes, who had just been elected the nation's nineteenth president, appointed him U.S. marshal of the District of Columbia. His job was to enforce federal laws in the U.S. capital.

The next year, Frederick and Anna moved to Washington DC. There, he purchased Cedar Hill, a house on nine acres (3.6 ha) in the Anacostia section of the city. Four years later, tragedy struck. On August 4, 1882, Anna died after suffering a stroke. The couple had been married for 44 years.

Douglass's marriage to Helen Pitts stirred controversy among both blacks and whites.

Controversial Second Marriage

On January 24, 1884, Douglass remarried. His new wife, Helen Pitts, was his former secretary, a white woman 20 years younger than he. Helen was the daughter of Gideon Pitts Jr., a dedicated abolitionist and Douglass's friend. Their marriage, however, caused uproars in both families, who opposed their interracial union.

Life and Times

In 1881, when Douglass was 63, he wrote his third autobiography, *Life and Times of Frederick Douglass.* The book shared details of Douglass's life that previously would have put him in danger.

Helen's family would no longer speak to her and forbade Frederick from entering their home. Frederick's children considered the marriage a great offense to their mother. Some of Douglass's friends also criticized him and refused to speak to him. A journalist for the *Pittsburgh Weekly News* wrote, "We have no further use for him [Douglass]. His picture hangs in our parlor, we will hang it in the stables."[2]

Others supported his decision. Black journalist Ida B. Wells wrote:

> *I, too, would have preferred that Mr. Douglass had chosen one of the beautiful, charming colored women of my race for his second wife. But he loved Helen Pitts . . . and it was outrageous that they should be crucified by both white and black people for doing so.*[3]

Despite the controversy, Frederick and Helen were happy together. In 1886 and 1887, they traveled to England, where they visited the people who had helped Douglass become a free man. Then, they visited France, Italy, Egypt, and Greece.

Minister to Haiti

In 1889, Douglass received a government appointment from newly elected President Benjamin Harrison. For two years, Douglass served as consul general, the U.S. minister, to Haiti. He resigned his position in 1891, however, because he objected to the way the U.S. government was using one of Haiti's port towns.

Return to the Eastern Shore

In June 1877, Douglass returned to Maryland's Eastern Shore. Memories flooded his mind when his steamer docked at St. Michaels for the first time in 41 years. On the streets, well-wishers greeted him and shook his hand. He made his way to the brick house beyond the large Wye mansion. There, he was escorted to the bedroom of Thomas Auld, his former master. Auld, now 82, was too ill to get out of bed. They greeted each other and mended a relationship that had been broken by the ugliness of slavery. Auld wept. Douglass, deeply moved, said, "I did not run away from you, but from slavery."[4]

Seventeen months later, Douglass again returned to the Eastern Shore. He visited Easton, where he had spent time in jail. Then, he made his way to Tuckahoe Creek, the place of his birth and the site of his grandmother Betsey's little log cabin. The cabin was no longer there, but Douglass did find the large cedar tree under which he had played as a child when he was "a spirited, joyous, uproarious, and happy boy."[5]

End of an Era

In his final years, Douglass never stopped speaking out for blacks who were legally free but were not treated equally. He also was an active defender of women's rights. On February 20, 1895, he spoke at a midday meeting of the National Women's Suffrage Association. On the platform with him was his longtime friend and suffragist, Susan B. Anthony. That evening at supper, Douglass discussed the meeting with his wife, lightheartedly mimicking some of the speakers. Suddenly he grasped his chest, fell to the floor, and died.

Telegrams of condolence arrived from U.S. politicians and leaders and dignitaries from all over the world. Douglass's funeral was held at the African Methodist Episcopal Church in Washington DC. His body was taken to Rochester, New York, where it lay in state until February 26. Douglass was buried at Mount Hope Cemetery next to his first wife, Anna, and his daughter, Annie.

The most prominent black man of the nineteenth century was gone. His death ended an era—a time when blacks were freed from centuries of slavery and given full citizenship in the United States. It was a time when black men received the right to vote and rose to government positions. Frederick Douglass led the way for future activists. He inspires those who continue to seek freedom and equality for all.

Frederick Douglass is remembered as one of the most brave and inspiring advocates for human rights in U.S. history.

Timeline

1818

Frederick Douglass is born in February.

1826

In March, Frederick is sent to live with the Hugh Auld family in Baltimore, where he learns to read.

1834

Frederick is sent to work as field hand for Edward Covey, the slave breaker, on January 1.

1838

In New Bedford, Massachusetts, Frederick Bailey changes his name to Frederick Douglass.

1842

Douglass is hired as an antislavery lecturer after his speaking tour draws large crowds.

1845

Narrative of the Life of Frederick Douglass, an American Slave is published in May.

1835	1836	1838
Frederick is assigned to the William Freeland farm; his escape plans are foiled.	Back in Baltimore, Frederick becomes an apprentice at the shipyards.	Frederick escapes to New York City on September 3; he marries Anna Murray soon after.

1845	1846	1847
Douglass sails to Europe for protection; he conducts speaking tours of Ireland, Scotland, and England.	British supporters pay Hugh Auld $711.66 for Douglass's freedom; Douglass is freed December 5.	The first issue of the *North Star* is published on December 3 in Rochester, New York.

Timeline

1859	1860	1861
Douglass flees to Canada and England to avoid arrest after the Harpers Ferry incident.	Douglass returns to the United States after receiving news of his daughter Annie's death.	The Civil War begins on April 12.

1877	1881	1882
Douglass is confirmed as U.S. marshal for the District of Columbia on March 17.	A third autobiography, *Life and Times of Frederick Douglass*, is published in November.	Anna dies on August 4.

1863	1863	1865
Lincoln signs the Emancipation Proclamation on January 1.	Douglass recruits black troops for the 54th Massachusetts Regiment; sons Lewis and Charles are among first to enlist.	The Civil War ends on April 9.

1884	1889	1895
Douglass marries Helen Pitts, a white woman and former secretary, on January 24.	Douglass is appointed minister to Haiti on July 1.	Douglass dies at Cedar Hill on February 20.

Essential Facts

Date of Birth

February 1818

Place of Birth

Tuckahoe, Maryland

Date of Death

February 20, 1895

Parents

Father: Unknown (Douglass believed he had a white father)

Mother: Harriet Bailey

Education

No formal education

Marriages

Anna Murray (1838–1882)

Helen Pitts (1884–1895)

Children

Rosetta (1839–1906), Lewis Henry (1840–1908), Frederick Jr. (1842–1892), Charles (1844–1920), Annie (1849–1860)

Career Highlights

Frederick Douglass is remembered as an eloquent public speaker and prolific writer of the abolitionist movement. He wrote three autobiographies: *Narrative of the Life of Frederick Douglass, an American Slave* (1845), *My Bondage and My Freedom* (1855), and *Life and Times of Frederick Douglass* (1881). With the help of his British admirers, he also started an antislavery newspaper, the *North Star*. During the Civil War, Douglass helped establish the Fifty-fourth Volunteer Massachusetts Regiment, an all-black regiment of the Union army. In his final years, Douglass served as U.S. marshal for the District of Columbia and U.S. Minister to Haiti.

Societal Contribution

Frederick Douglass is one of the most influential African Americans in U.S. history. This renowned speaker, author, and abolitionist dedicated his life to emancipation and equality for blacks, women, and all people.

Conflicts

Frederick Douglass's life was rife with conflict. As a slave, he watched gruesome whippings and was beaten himself. After a failed attempt to run away from the Freeland Farm, he was literally dragged through the town. Then, as a fugitive, he faced the constant danger of being caught and returned South. Later in life, Douglass fled the country after he was issued an arrest warrant for his connection to John Brown and the Virginia Harpers Ferry raid. After decades of speaking out for equal rights for blacks and whites, Douglass stirred controversy in the last years of his life when he married Helen Pitts, his white secretary.

Quote

"It may be that my misery in slavery will only increase my happiness when I get free. There is a better day coming."—*Frederick Douglass*

Additional Resources

Select Bibliography

Blight, David W. *Beyond the Battlefield: Race, Memory, and the American Civil War*. Amherst, MA: University of Massachusetts Press, 2002.

Dawes, James. *The Language of War*. Cambridge, MA: Harvard University Press, 2005.

Frederick Douglass Autobiographies [Narrative of the Life of Frederick Douglass, an American Slave; My Bondage and My Freedom; Life and Times of Frederick Douglass]. New York, NY: Literary Classics of the United States, Inc., 1994.

Gilder Lehrman Institute of American History. *Frederick Douglass from Slavery to Freedom: The Journey to New York City [Educator's Guide]*. New York, NY: Gilder Lehrman Institute of American History. p. 5. 19 July 2009 <http://www.lorenzoculturalcenter.com/PDFs/EG-Frederick-Douglass.pdf>.

Halpern, Rick, and Enrico Dal Lago, eds. *Slavery and Emancipation*. Hoboken, NJ: Wiley-Blackwell, 2002.

McFeely, William S. *Frederick Douglass*. New York, NY: Norton, 1991.

Washington, Booker T. *Frederick Douglass*. Philadelphia, PA: Jacobs, 1906.

Wu, Jin-Ping. *Frederick Douglass and the Black Liberation Movement. The North Star of American Blacks.* New York, NY: Garland, 2000.

Further Reading

Ruffin, Frances E. *Frederick Douglass: A Powerful Voice for Freedom.* New York, NY: Sterling, 2008.

Stanley, George E. *Frederick Douglass: Abolitionist Hero.* New York, NY: Aladdin, 2008.

Yancey, Diane. *Frederick Douglass*. San Diego, CA: Lucent Books, 2003.

Web Links

To learn more about Frederick Douglass, visit ABDO Publishing Company online at **www.abdopublishing.com**. Web sites about Frederick Douglass are featured on our Book Links page. These links are routinely monitored and updated to provide the most current information available.

Places to Visit

The Frederick Douglass National Historic Site
Cedar Hill, 1411 W Street, SE, Washington DC 20020
202-426-5961
www.nps.gov/FRDO/index.htm
Cedar Hill, the home of Frederick Douglass from 1877 until his death in 1895, displays and preserves Douglass's legacy and his efforts to abolish slavery.

The Historical Society of Talbot County Museum & Gardens
Frederick Douglass Driving Tour of Talbot County
25 South Washington Street, Easton, MD 21601
410-822-0773
www.hstc.org/toursandmuseum.htm#Tours
Self-guided driving tour of 14 sites related to Frederick Douglass's life in Talbot County, Maryland, both as a slave and later as a free man.

Glossary

abolitionist
A person dedicated to ending slavery.

apprentice
A person who works for a skilled worker for a period of time to learn a trade.

communal
Shared by a group of people or a community.

Confederates
People from the states that seceded from the United States at the start of the Civil War and made up the Confederate States of America.

domestic servant
A slave who worked inside his or her owner's home, caring for children, cleaning, cooking, and doing other household chores.

emancipation
The freeing of a person from slavery or bondage.

inaugurate
To formally begin someone's term in public office, such as the presidency.

orator
A skilled public speaker.

overseer
A supervisor who kept watch over someone's slaves and directed their work.

peninsula
A piece of land that projects into a body of water and is connected to the mainland by a strip of land.

retaliation
Action taken against someone as payback for an injury or evil.

secede
To withdraw, or separate, from a country or another group.

seine

A large fishing net made to hang vertically in the water with weights on the lower edge; to fish with such a net.

suffrage

The right or privilege to vote.

tainted

Affected by rot or decay.

Underground Railroad

The secret network of people who helped runaway slaves reach sanctuary in a free state or Canada.

Union

States in the North that fought against the South in the Civil War.

Source Notes

Chapter 1. The Slave Breaker

1. Frederick Douglass. *Frederick Douglass Autobiographies*. New York, NY: Literary Classics of the United States, 1994. 259.
2. Ibid. 263.
3. Ibid. 264.
4. Ibid. 58.
5. Ibid. 58.
6. Ibid. 268.
7. Ibid. 269.
8. Ibid. 60.

Chapter 2. Born a Slave

1. Frederick Douglass. *Frederick Douglass Autobiographies*. New York, NY: Literary Classics of the United States, 1994. 477.
2. Anthony Papers, Item 97, Ledger Book "B." Quoted in Dickson J. Preston. *Young Frederick Douglass: The Maryland Years*. Baltimore, MD: The Johns Hopkins University Press, 1980. 18.
3. Frederick Douglass. *Frederick Douglass Autobiographies*. New York, NY: Literary Classics of the United States, 1994. 476.
4. Ibid. 24.
5. Ibid. 145.
6. Ibid. 150.
7. Ibid. 16.
8. Ibid. 150.
9. Ibid. 24.

Chapter 3. The Slave and the Whip

1. Frederick Douglass. *Frederick Douglass Autobiographies*. New York, NY: Literary Classics of the United States, 1994. 186.
2. Ibid. 33.
3. Dickson J. Preston. *Young Frederick Douglass: The Maryland Years*. Baltimore, MD: The Johns Hopkins University Press, 1980. 66.
4. Frederick Douglass. *Frederick Douglass Autobiographies*. New York, NY: Literary Classics of the United States, 1994. 499.
5. David W. Blight. *Beyond the Battlefield: Race, Memory, and the American Civil War*. Amherst, MA: University of Massachusetts Press, 2002. 11.

Chapter 4. Baltimore
1. Frederick Douglass. *Frederick Douglass Autobiographies*. New York, NY: Literary Classics of the United States, 1994. 36.
2. Ibid. 239.
3. Ibid. 237.

Chapter 5. Motivated to Learn
1. Frederick Douglass. *Frederick Douglass Autobiographies*. New York, NY: Literary Classics of the United States, 1994. 216.
2. Ibid. 217.
3. Ibid. 217.
4. Ibid. 218.
5. Rick Halpern and Enrico Dal Lago. *Slavery and Emancipation*. Hoboken, NJ: Wiley-Blackwell, 2002. 298.
6. Ibid. 297–298.
7. Frederick Douglass. *Frederick Douglass Autobiographies*. New York, NY: Literary Classics of the United States, 1994. 44.

Chapter 6. Return to Slavery
1. Frederick Douglass. *Frederick Douglass Autobiographies*. New York, NY: Literary Classics of the United States, 1994. 560.
2. Ibid. 286.
3. Ibid. 77.
4. Ibid. 78.
5. Frederick Douglass. *Narrative of the Life of Frederick Douglass, an American Slave, Written by Himself.* New York, NY: Dell Publishing, 1997. 90.

Source Notes Continued

Chapter 7. Escape to New York
1. Frederick Douglass. *Frederick Douglass Autobiographies.* New York, NY: Literary Classics of the United States, 1994. 328.
2. Gilder Lehrman Institute of American History. *Frederick Douglass from Slavery to Freedom: The Journey to New York City [Educator's Guide]*. New York, NY: Gilder Lehrman Institute of American History. 19 July 2009 <http://www.lorenzoculturalcenter.com/PDFs/EG-Frederick-Douglass.pdf>.
3. Frederick Douglass. "My Escape from Slavery." *Page by Page Books*. 9 Nov. 2009 <http://www.pagebypagebooks.com/Frederick_Douglass/My_Escape_From_Slavery/My_Escape_From_Slavery_p1.html>.

Chapter 8. Popular Orator
1. Frederick Douglass. *Frederick Douglass Autobiographies.* New York, NY: Literary Classics of the United States, 1994. 94.
2. Ibid.
3. "William Lloyd Garrison papers: 1833–1882." *Massachusetts Historical Society*. 20 July 2009 <http://www.masshist.org/findingaids/doc.cfm?fa=fa0278#citation>.
4. George W. Williams. *History of the Negro Race in America from 1619 to 1880.* Vol. II. New York, NY: G.P. Putnam's Sons, 1883. 23 July 2009. <http://books.google.com/books?id=eWQFAAAAQAAJ&pg=PR1&dq=hugh+auld+jr+children&source=gbs_selected_pages&cad=5>.
5. Frederick Douglass. "The Meaning of July Fourth for the Negro." *PBS*. 23 July 2009 <http://www.pbs.org/wgbh/aia/part4/4h2927t.html>.
6. Frederick Douglass. *Frederick Douglass Autobiographies.* New York, NY: Literary Classics of the United States, 1994. 763.

Chapter 9. War!
1. Abraham Lincoln and Stephen Arnold Douglas. *Political Debates Between Abraham Lincoln and Stephen A. Douglas*. Cleveland, OH: The Burrows Brothers Company, 1894. 315.
2. James Dawes. *The Language of War*. Cambridge, MA: Harvard University Press, 2005. 20.
3. Abraham Lincoln. "The Emancipation Proclamation." January 1, 1863. Washington, DC: National Archives and Records Administration. 21 July 2009 <http://www.archives.gov/exhibits/featured_documents/emancipation_proclamation/transcript.html>.
4. Garrett Epps. *Democracy Reborn: The Fourteenth Amendment and the Fight for Equal Rights in Post-Civil War America*. New York, NY: Holt Paperbacks, 2007. 156.
5. Rick Halpern and Enrico Dal Lago. *Slavery and Emancipation*. Hoboken, NJ: Wiley-Blackwell, 2002. 382.
6. David B. Chesebrough. *Frederick Douglass: Oratory from Slavery*. Westport, CT: Greenwood Press, 1998. 62.
7. "13th Amendment to the U.S. Constitution." *The Library of Congress*. 22 July 2009 <http://www.loc.gov/rr/program/bib/ourdocs/13thamendment.html>.

Chapter 10. Milestones
1. "15th Amendment to the Constitution." *Primary Documents in American History. The Library of Congress*. 22 July 2009 <http://www.loc.gov/rr/program/bib/ourdocs/15thamendment.html>.
2. Linda O. McMurry. *To Keep the Waters Troubled: The Life of Ida B. Wells*. Oxford, UK: Oxford University Press, 2000. 185.
3. Ibid. 185.
4. Booker T. Washington. *Frederick Douglass*. Philadelphia, PA: George W. Jacobs & Company, 1906. 328.
5. Frederick Douglass. *Frederick Douglass Autobiographies*. New York, NY: Literary Classics of the United States, 1994. 145.

Index

Anthony, Aaron, 15, 17, 20, 24–27, 30, 31, 38, 51
Auld, Hugh, 31, 35, 36, 38, 40, 43–44, 48, 58, 61, 63, 66, 75
Auld, Lucretia, 30–32, 36, 38
Auld, Rowena, 48, 50
Auld, Sophia, 31, 35–36, 37, 39, 40, 43–45, 61, 63
Auld, Thomas, 30–31, 38, 40, 48, 50–51, 52, 54, 58, 75, 93
Auld, Tommy, 32, 35, 40, 43, 45, 61
Aunt Hester, 26–27, 39
Aunt Katy, 28, 31, 39

Bailey, Arianna (sister), 16
Bailey, Betsey (grandmother), 15, 16, 17, 18, 20–21, 39
Bailey, Eliza (sister), 15, 18, 20, 39, 51
Bailey, Harriet (mother), 14, 15, 16, 21
Bailey, Henry, 55–58
Bailey, Kitty (sister), 16
Bailey, Perry (brother), 15, 18, 20, 39, 40, 82
Bailey, Sarah (sister), 15, 20
Baltimore clippers, 36, 64
Brown, John, 77–78

Cedar Hill, 90
Civil War, 9, 78, 80–85
Covey, Edward, 7–12, 51–54, 62

Demby, Bill, 25, 26
Douglass, Anna (wife, first), 65–66, 67–68, 71, 73, 74, 76, 90, 94
Douglass, Annie (daughter, second), 76, 78, 94
Douglass, Charles (son, fourth), 74, 84, 89
Douglass, Frederick
Baltimore years, 34–48
birth, 14
childhood, 16–18
death, 94
escapes from slavery, 12, 55–58, 66–68
family, 15–16, 71, 74, 76
freedom, 75
grave, 94
political candidate, 89
reading, 43–45
shipyards, 61–65
slave breaker, 7–12, 51–54
U.S. marshal, 90
U.S. minister to Haiti, 93
Wye plantation years, 21–31
Douglass, Frederick Jr. (son, second), 74
Douglass, Helen Pitts, (wife, second), 90, 91–92
Douglass, Lewis Henry (son, first), 71, 84
Douglass, Rosetta (daughter, first), 71, 73

East Baltimore Mental Improvement Society, 65
Emancipation Proclamation, 82–83

Fifteenth Amendment, 88–89
Fifty-fourth Massachusetts Volunteer Infantry Regiment, 84–85
Fourteenth Amendment, 88
Freeland, William, 54, 55, 57, 58

Garrison, William Lloyd, 45–46, 47, 65, 72, 73
Gore, Austin, 25, 26

Harris, Henry, 55–58
Harris, John, 55–58

Jenkins, Sandy, 53, 55

Liberator, 46, 47, 72
Life and Times of Frederick Douglass, 92
Lincoln, Abraham, 38, 81–82, 85–86
Lloyd, Daniel, 30
Lloyd, Edward, 15, 18, 20, 24, 30

Massachusetts Anti-Slavery Society, 73
Murray, Anna. *See* Douglass, Anna

Narrative of the Life of Frederick Douglass, an American Slave, 10, 74
North Star, 75–77, 89

"Path to Freedom" Walking Tour, Baltimore, 38
Pennington, James W. C., 67

Roberts, Charles, 55–56

slave auctions, 15, 39–40
slave songs, 21
slave trade, 45–46, 57–58, 64
slavery,
  end of, 82–83, 86, 88
  practice of, 9

Thirteenth Amendment, 86

Underground Railroad, 9, 47, 67

Wye House, 19–20
  plantation life, 17, 27–29

About the Author

Sue Vander Hook has been writing and editing books for 20 years. Her writing career began with several nonfiction books for adults and moved to a focus on educational books for children and young adults. She especially enjoys writing about historical events and biographies of people who made a difference. Her published works include a high school curriculum and series on disease, technology, and sports. Sue lives with her family in Minnesota.

Photo Credits

AP Images, cover, 3, 80, 83, 95, 99 (top), 99 (bottom); Red Line Editorial, 6, 60; David Duprey/AP Images, 13; North Wind Picture Archives, 14, 23, 24, 34, 41, 62, 96 (top); Kathleen Lange/AP Images, 19; Corbis, 29; Louie Psihoyos/Corbis, 49; Bettmann/Corbis, 56; Samuel J. Miller/AP Images, 59, 98; Michael Okoniewski/AP Images, 70

Photos Courtesy National Park Service, Museum Management Program and Frederick Douglass National Historic Site: Frederick Douglass, FRDO2169/http://www.nps.gov/history/museum/exhibits/frdo/exb/visionary/FRDO2169_FRDOyoung.html, 33; William Lloyd Garrison, FRDO3124/http://www.nps.gov/history/museum/exhibits/frdo/exb/powerIdea/FRDO3124.html, 42; *Narrative of the Life of Frederick Douglass,* FRDO10995/Photo by Carol M. Highsmith/http://www.nps.gov/history/museum/exhibits/frdo/exb/mightyWord/FRDO10995_bookNarrative.jpg, 50, 96 (bottom); Mrs. Anna Douglass, FRDO246/Photo by Carol M. Highsmith/http://www.nps.gov/history/museum/exhibits/frdo/exb/homeinWashington/FRDO246_annaDouglass.html, 69; Rosetta Douglass, FRDO4812/http://www.nps.gov/history/museum/exhibits/frdo/exb/homeinWashington/frdo4812.html, 72; *The North Star,* 1847–1850, FRDO3219/http://www.nps.gov/history/museum/exhibits/frdo/exb/mightyWord/frdo3219_north_star_newspap.html, 79, 97; Letter from the Department of the Interior, FRDO3863/http://www.nps.gov/history/museum/exhibits/frdo/exb/visionary/frdo3863_letter_Lincoln_sig.html, 87; Frederick Douglass in His Study at Cedar Hill, FRDO3886/http://www.nps.gov/history/museum/exhibits/frdo/exb/visionary/FRDO3886.html, 88; Helen Pitts Douglass (1838–1903), FRDO2814/http://www.nps.gov/history/museum/exhibits/frdo/exb/womensRights/frdo2814_helen_pitts_dougla.html, 91